Circles

Teddy Borth

Abdo
SHAPES ARE FUN!
Kids

abdopublishing.com

Published by Abdo Kids, a division of ABDO, PO Box 398166, Minneapolis, Minnesota 55439.
Copyright © 2016 by Abdo Consulting Group, Inc. International copyrights reserved in all countries.
No part of this book may be reproduced in any form without written permission from the publisher.

Printed in the United States of America, North Mankato, Minnesota.

102015

012016

THIS BOOK CONTAINS
RECYCLED MATERIALS

Photo Credits: Getty Images, iStock, Shutterstock

Production Contributors: Teddy Borth, Jennie Forsberg, Grace Hansen

Design Contributors: Candice Keimig, Dorothy Toth

Library of Congress Control Number: 2015941975

Cataloging-in-Publication Data

Borth, Teddy.

 Circles / Teddy Borth.

   p. cm. -- (Shapes are fun!)

ISBN 978-1-68080-142-2 (lib. bdg.)

Includes index.

1. Circles--Juvenile literature. 2. Geometry--Juvenile literature. 3. Shapes--Juvenile literature.   I. Title.

516/.152--dc23

                        2015941975

Table of Contents

Circles 4

Count the Circles! . . .22

Glossary. 23

Index 24

Abdo Kids Code. 24

Circles

A circle is round. The length from its edge to the center is always the same.

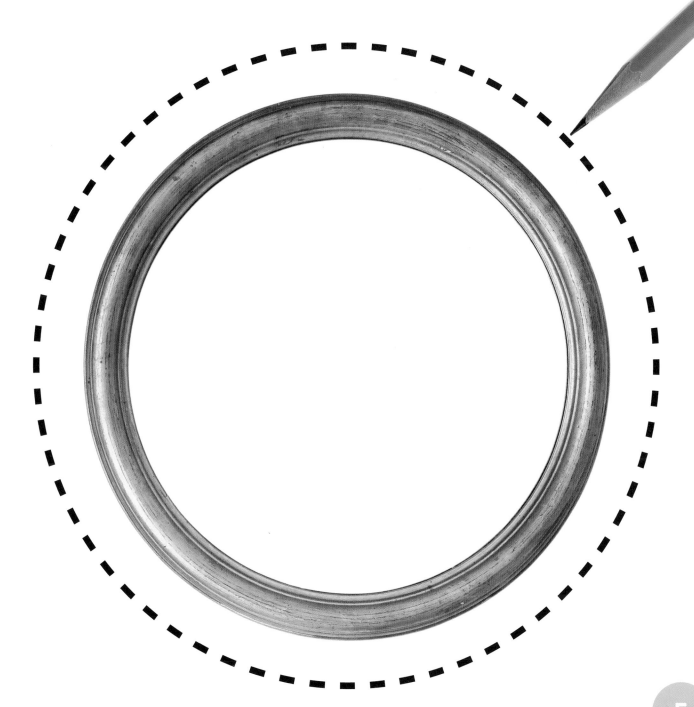

This shape is found all over!

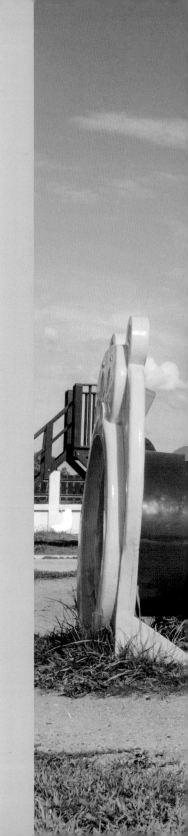

They are on wheels.

Cars use wheels.

Jugglers use them.

They call them rings.

They are on food.

Max's family loves pizza!

Circles show time.

They are found on clocks.

Hula hoops are circles. Fran can keep it spinning for 5 minutes!

Circles are on money.

Liz counts her coins.

Look around you!

You will find a circle.

Count the Circles!

Glossary

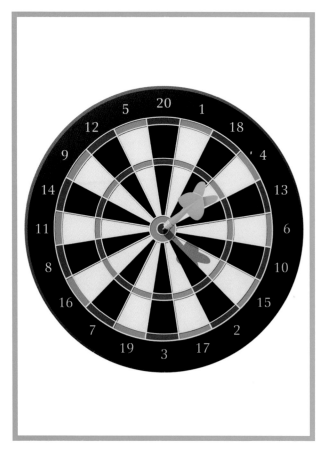

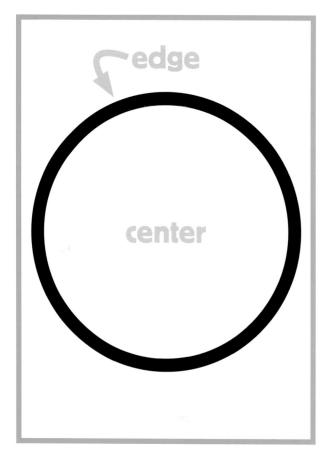

center
the point inside a circle that is an equal distance from any point on the edge.

edge
the line where an object begins or ends.

Index

car 8

clock 14

coins 18

food 12

hula hoop 16

juggler 10

length 4

pizza 12

ring 10

wheel 8

abdokids.com

Use this code to log on to abdokids.com and access crafts, games, videos, and more!

Abdo Kids Code:
SCK1422